MANIFESTED
Plans

God Leads,
You Follow

Nanette-Michelle Smith

WESTBOW
PRESS®
A DIVISION OF THOMAS NELSON
& ZONDERVAN

This book is a work of non-fiction. Unless otherwise noted, the author and the publisher make no explicit guarantees as to the accuracy of the information contained in this book and in some cases, names of people and places have been altered to protect their privacy.

WestBow Press books may be ordered through booksellers or by contacting:

WestBow Press
A Division of Thomas Nelson & Zondervan
1663 Liberty Drive
Bloomington, IN 47403
www.westbowpress.com
844-714-3454

Because of the dynamic nature of the Internet, any web addresses or links contained in this book may have changed since publication and may no longer be valid. The views expressed in this work are solely those of the author and do not necessarily reflect the views of the publisher, and the publisher hereby disclaims any responsibility for them.

Any people depicted in stock imagery provided by Getty Images are models, and such images are being used for illustrative purposes only. Certain stock imagery © Getty Images.

All Scripture quotations are taken from the King James Version.

ISBN: 978-1-6642-0972-5 (sc)
ISBN: 978-1-6642-0971-8 (e)

Library of Congress Control Number: 2020920737

Print information available on the last page.

WestBow Press rev. date: 10/29/2020

CHAPTER 1

The Introduction

Imagine God manifesting Himself in your life. Imagine Him manifesting in all your plans and changed behavior. This could be the beginning of a new you. Not just any new you but a powerful new you. Be careful. Going down this road, you just might discover who God is. You might just find who God actually created you to be. You might just uncover your true purpose. This can change everything.

Think about when you make plans. When you get encouraged to make life-changing plans. Allowing God to take control of these plans can open doors that you thought were *impossible* to open. Anything can be everything when God is involved. Matthew 19:26 says, "With men this is impossible, but with God all things are possible."

Now that we have a better understanding, let's get down to business. Let's start at square one: *the idea*. An idea is a thought or suggestion as to a possible course of action; an aim or purpose. I am sure you have a lot of ideas. I am also sure that you have had this one idea that keeps finding its way to the surface. Even when you are trying to entertain other ideas that you may have had interest in, there is always that one idea that can't seem to expire. Let's say you gave that lingering idea a chance. OK. Now it's here. Sitting in your mind. Frontline. Now what? What is the next step? Write it down?

Absolutely. But before you write it down, you have to pray about it. You have to pray about *everything*. In the Bible, 1 Thessalonians 5:16 says, "Pray without ceasing." Praying is how we spiritually connect and communicate with God. Remember: we are spirits with bodies and not bodies with spirits. Our Creator loves when we spiritually communicate with Him. Ceasing means to put an end to something. So to pray *without* ceasing means to constantly pray about everything.

This is another door for God to go through to manifest Himself in your life, your plans, and your ideas.

NOTES

CHAPTER 2

Plans including God

When I was younger, I always wanted to be a singer, but I loved track and field. I loved running the eight hundred meters and the four-by-four-hundred-meter relay. Those were my two favorite races. I made it to the Junior Olympics for the four-hundred-meter race and the four-by-four-hundred-meter relay. I just knew my plan to be a track star was going to succeed, but things took a quick left when I turned seventeen. I was diagnosed with scoliosis. Scoliosis is a medical condition in which a person's spine has a sideways curve, usually forming an S or a C shape. I had to go into surgery. I had to learn to walk all over again. The doctor told my family it can take a couple of months to fully heal. Through the grace of God, I was out of the hospital, fully walking, a week after my surgery. I got home and carefully sat on my couch, thinking about those plans I'd had of being a track star. I knew that that plan was now tainted.

Sometimes, we make plans and don't include God or even take into consideration if that's what He wanted us to do. What if that was not God's plan for my life? So things had to shift. Jeremiah 1:5 says, "Before I formed thee in the belly, I knew thee." So God already knew our purpose before we were even physically thought of. What about Psalm 37:23? "The steps of a good man are ordered by the Lord, and he delighteth in His way." God only wants what is best for us, and He designed us perfectly. "Be ye therefore perfect even as Father which is in Heaven is perfect" (Matthew 5:48). If the Bible tells us that we are made perfectly, then why cannot we trust our Creator to know what plan He specifically designed us for? This is why is you should always pray and include God in your plans. Ask Him first. "God, is this the way *You* want me to go?" You can even tell God your plans. That is another way of keeping Him in the loop. Although God already knows, it is the effort that is appreciated. Proverbs 3:6 says, "In all ways acknowledge Him, and He will direct your path."

Therefore, let's consult with God from now on. Lean not on your own understanding because even when God the Almighty is involved, He can and may use things, people, etc., you least expect to play a major part of the plan He has for you. It will all fall perfectly into place.

NOTES

CHAPTER 3

Self-Esteem

Genesis 1:27 says, "So God created man in His own image, in the image God created He him." Who are you? OK. Let's ask that question from another angle. Who do you think you are? How do you feel about who you think you are? Do other opinions about you assist in how you feel about yourself? These are upfront and straightforward questions you have to ask yourself. As a matter of fact, when was the last time you looked in the mirror?

Try this. Go to the mirror, and look directly at yourself. This time, let's not fix our hair or check how our outfits fit our bodies. Let's actually pretend that our bodies are not even present. Look into your eyes, and simply say hello. If you looked deep into your eyes while excluding the physical you, you have just spoken to your spirit. You should be able to feel the difference. That is who you are. That is who God communicates with.

While still staring at your spirit, your "real you," begin to recite to yourself who God says you are. Need help? Let's look at Ephesians 1:4. "According as He hath chosen us in Him before the foundation of the world, that we should be holy and without blame before Him in love." John 15:16 says, "You didn't choose God, He chose you." So you are chosen!

Say you were out shopping and knew the exact pair of heels you were looking for before you ever saw them. Then *bam!* There they were front and center in a department store in the mall. You rush in there with no hesitation at all. Full of certainty. You pay a *major* price for them. You don't even think twice about the cost. You pay full price for these specific heels. Now you have your heels, and you are feeling exceptional, high maintenance, and proud. You love these shoes so much that you protect them with your life. No one can touch these shoes. No scratches can appear on them because that will upset you. Theses shoes are for a purpose. They were chosen. They're loved and fully paid for.

That is how God looks at you. *You.* You are chosen. You are loved. You have a purpose. You are fully paid for at the highest price.

John 3:16 says, "FOR GOD SO LOVED THE WORLD (you) THAT HE GAVE HIS ONLY BEGOTTEN SON (the price) THAT WHOSEVER BELIEVES IN HIM SHOULD NOT PERISH, BUT HAVE EVERLASTING LIFE (the purpose)."

NOTES

CHAPTER 4

Distractions

Distraction: A thing or things that prevent us from giving full attention to something else; an extreme agitation of the mind or emotion.

Have you ever been focused on something and thought that this thought was really great? You start feeding off this great thought. Ideas start rushing through. You begin to get all excited. Fearless. Courageous. Ready, even. Then suddenly, you receive a text message from, for example, a friend you haven't heard from in a long time and you have been meaning to call this person just to check in. See how he or she is doing and all. Now you're excited about texting your friend back to let him or her know how you have been meaning to call and how much you guys need to catch up. Meanwhile, your first thought, that idea that you thought was so great, shrinks into a tiny little box and is pushed to the back of your mind. The reason is now you are excited about something else.

When you focus on something, it most likely shares a stingy space. In other words, tunnel vision. Tunnel vision is the tendency to focus exclusively on a single or limited goal or point of view. It's a defective sight in which an object cannot be properly seen if it is not close to the center of the field or view. So now your great thought or idea is that object that cannot be seen because it is not the center of attention anymore. You know that it's there, but since it's just a thought, it's not as important as something you can physically see and respond to.

When you are just creating an idea, it's not tangible. It's abstract. Abstract is an existing thought or idea without a physical or concrete existence. By your thought or idea being in such an abstract form, it is easier for it to disappear in your mind. You have to take hold of it. Grab it as soon as you think about it. Check with God about it. Keep Him in the loop. Then write it down along with other great thoughts that were feeding off that great thought or idea.

When this type of spark occurs, you have to learn how to recognize and ignore distractions. It can also be the devil in disguise trying to throw you off your game because he knows it can be something God can bless or even multiply.

The devil does not want you to have what God has for you. He will always try to distract you from the truth. In this case, the truth is that you are a powerful being full of greatness and good ideas that can change the world for the better. Learn that, manifest in that, and stay away from distractions. Learn how to put your distractions on hold and have tunnel vision for your vision. When a great thought comes to mind, put the distractions on hold, put that text message on hold, and put those Facebook and Instagram notifications on hold. One thing for sure is that those things are always going to be right there. You can go back to those anytime. Your great idea can fade away in a second, due to lack of focus. Let's stay focused.

NOTES

CHAPTER 5

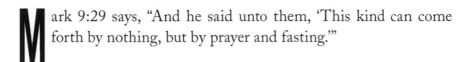

Mark 9:29 says, "And he said unto them, 'This kind can come forth by nothing, but by prayer and fasting.'"

> **Fasting**: abstaining from all or some kinds of food or drink, especially as a religion observance.

> **Prayer**: a solemn request for help or expression of thanks addressed to God.

Prayer and fasting are the two most important things we can do as followers of Christ. It helps us tap into our spiritual selves. Galatians 5:16 says, "This I say then, walk in the spirit, and ye shall not fulfill the lust of the flesh." Verse 22 of Galatians explains the spirit by saying, "But the fruit of the spirit is love, joy, peace, longsuffering, gentleness, goodness, faith." Verse 23 adds, "Meekness, temperance: against such there is no law." Living in the spirit is one of the ultimate goals, and it is easier to communicate with the Father through spirit. When we are fasting, we are activating that spirit realm.

For the ones who don't quite comprehend fasting, it is more for a biblical purpose. Fasting goes hand in hand with prayer. When you decide to fast, make sure it is for a biblical purpose and not for a selfish purpose such as wanting to fast for a lot of money as opposed to fasting for a stronger prayer connection with God. See the difference? You wouldn't have to fast for things like money if you are in search of Christ. Philippians 4:19 says, "But my God shall supply all your need according to his riches and glory by Jesus Christ." Your needs and beyond will be met when you follow Jesus Christ.

Even sacrificing one small meal can be considered a fast. It's just the purpose of the fast and what you will be praying for during the fast. This is a strong way to get closer to Jesus: fasting and praying for a biblical purpose.

The thing is you want to be close *to* God, and you want to be close *with* God. You want to learn to walk in the spirit to be closer to God. What's even more of the benefit of fasting and praying is now you are actually seeking the Father. Matthew 6:33 says, "But seek ye first the kingdom of God, and His righteousness; and all these things shall be added unto you." By fasting and praying, you are volunteering to seek God. And the Bible says, as you just read the verse from Matthew, that when you seek God, everything else you need will follow.

What other great time it would be to introduce your plans to God, in the midst of you being in the spirit with him, while fasting and praying. I dare you to include God in your plans while you are in His presence. I bet you will find out that He is a living God who overcomes the impossible and wins. Do this at your own risk. What are you waiting for? Your life awaits you.

NOTES

CHAPTER 6

Trust in the Lord

Trust. What is trust? Trust is a firm belief in the reliability, truth, ability, or strength of someone or something. Now this is no secret that trust can be misused. It can scar a person if it is mishandled. Oftentimes when we experience misused trust, that kind of opens this door of withdrawal, right? We kind of just pull away. In most cases, since we have had a history of our trust being taken advantage of, it gets easier to detach from the people who misused our trust. We all know that man will fail you, right? If that were not true, then why does the Bible state in Psalm 118:8, "It's better to trust in the Lord, then to put confidence in men"? We are not talking strictly on man as in the gender but man as in humankind. God knew this. In the beginning, neither Adam nor Eve could not hold trust with God when they both decided to disobey Him in the Garden of Eden by eating the forbidden fruit. That was the start of it all.

What about God? Can we trust God? Of course we can. God has proven the ultimate showing us how down He was for us by allowing His only Son to lay down His life for *us*. Jesus never broke trust. Not with man or with God.

Moving on. Now that we have a depth understanding about trust, let's see what God wants us to do with trust, seeing that man can't hold his own but God can. This is telling us that we can trust God with our plans. Proverbs 3:5 says, "Trust in the Lord with all thine heart, and lean not onto your own understanding."

Am I the only one who feels like, or experiences when I put matters into my own understanding, things turn out wrong? An example is relationships. I was attracted to the type of boys who had this "thuglike" mentality. The boys who thought they had to act extra hardcore and aggressive to prove their manhood. Every time I took those types of boys seriously, I came out with the same results. First, these boys always seemed to look for their mothers in their women. Second, they depended on their pride to keep themselves alive and safe, and honestly, it caused them to be paranoid like the whole world was against them. I found myself in cycles. I just wanted love. The thing was I was putting trust in men to fill a void. The whole time it was God's love that I needed. I was craving a type of love that could not have been completed by men. Only God. I had to put my trust in God.

When I finally let go and let God, He showed up and showed out. He filled me with this overflowing feeling of His love. This love was a feeling of real love. I've experienced the real love of God, and I still do. I knew it was His love because I never felt this kind of love before, but somehow, I knew it was a form of love. This love also included an overflow of confidence, of trust, and of the ability to manifest more of that feeling, free from God. All I had to do was trust in God. He knew.

Put all your trust into God, and watch what He does. He just needs faith from you—faith as small as a mustard seed—to manifest Himself and bloom in your life. Take away putting trust in men and flesh, and trust in Jesus Christ, our Lord and Savior.

NOTES

CHAPTER 7

God Will Allow Manifestation

He who has my commandments and keeps them, it is he who loves me. And he who loves me will be loved by my Father, and I will love him and manifest Myself to him.

—John 14:21

God has to be invited into your life, into your heart, and into your plans before He can manifest Himself in your favor. You have to invite God into your world. God knows everything. He knows what you need before you even notice you need it. Matthew 6:8 says, "Therefore, do not be like them. For your Father knows the things you have need of before you ask Him." Remember who God is before you try to comprehend what He is capable of. This is the living God who created the whole world and life itself in six days! There is nothing too big or too complicated for our God.

A plan can seem so far out, especially when we first come up with it. After we write it down and stand back and read it, it can look far out, as if we are asking for too much time consumption of our lives. It may even seem too big to accomplish. That is normally what happens when we are looking at things with a carnal mind and not thinking about God. See? Right there at that moment of doubt is when you can invite God into your plans. Seeing that we are dealing with the God who created the universe, I am sure He can help put your plan together. The more we remember who God is, the easier it is for us to understand what He is capable of.

God can work in mysterious ways when we give Him the green light to manifest Himself in our plans and in our lives. Things will start "magically" falling into place. During this process, it can get a little complicated for us because we might lose or gain friends, or opportunities we might feel were right in *our* timing might not go through. That doesn't mean our plans are not getting handled correctly in God's hands. But He can be moving things around, taking away things, and adding things that He sees fit for the plan to succeed. It simply means that God sees the worth in us and in our plans. He knows whose hands to propose your plans to. We have to trust God. He sees what we can't see.

Allowing God to manifest Himself in our plans is the best thing for us to do, especially if we want success in our plans and in our lives in general.

NOTES

CHAPTER 8

Finding Love in Jesus

Making plans can be very difficult sometimes. Honestly, it can be very time-consuming. Time can seem like it can be fast-forwarding. Next thing you know, friends and family start complaining about how you are not spending the usual time with them, but you don't have that same craving anymore. Not like you used to. Ever since you have allowed God to manifest Himself in your favor, you have a different craving. This craving provides a different taste for a different type of food, such as praise, alone time with God, and accomplishment.

During this alone time, God is in your presence, teaching you what His type of love is. This type of love is a very important ingredient. First John 4:7–8 says, "Beloved, let us love one another, for love is from God, and whoever loves has been born of God and knows God. Anyone who does not love, does not know God, because God is love."

When we spend time with God, He is teaching us to be more like Him. Also, He is teaching us the right way to treat others. Love is a great way to change the energy. Love can change people. It can even cause people to love themselves more, enough to push through their lives. We never know who's going through something, and just a small ounce of love might be exactly what they needed in that moment to lift up. Lift up enough to feel good about themselves again.

Now this can be important. God taught you to love, so you go out and love. You can show love to others, and they might want to show appreciation in return. This appreciation can be (watch this) a connection they just remembered they had, that can help that same plan of yours that you let God manifest in. Remember God can move mysteriously sometimes. So now that person you showed godly love to shows you appreciation by helping you with your plan. Now your plan is in the right hands, and you can feel that it is right because there was no effort on your behalf. You can just feel that God did that. He always let it be known because He is not a God of confusion.

Always show love to one another. You never know who God is using in your favor.

NOTES

CHAPTER 9

The Execution

W e have talked about understanding who God is. We have dissected what manifestation is. We have covered plans and distractions, self-esteem, love, and fasting and praying over our plans. Lastly, we went over allowing God to manifest Himself by openly inviting Him into our lives. You now have all the ingredients you need to execute your vision.

You have a vision that you strongly feel will fulfill a sense of accomplishment in this life. It's now time to execute your plan. At this point, make sure to repeat the ingredients you have learned as a daily saying, daily belief, daily faith, and daily routine. Your success will become easier as you climb up the ladder of blessings. Don't be surprised if your finances increase. That comes with the package of allowing God to manifest Himself.

Your life can change. It can change for the better. God can put you in positions to be able to help others and to share your ingredients for others to eat too.

Now get up and go be successful in Jesus's name.

CHAPTER 10

The Testimony

My name is Nanette Michelle Smith. I am allowing God to manifest Himself in this book. I want to use this last chapter to share my testimony and how God brought me through.

Growing up in the city of Compton, California, was not the easiest for me. I literally had to fight for my survival though junior high and high school. I mean girls would find the most invalid reasons to fight me. I would always have to fight more than two to three people at a time. I was in and out of different schools because my behavior was bad. I was molested, raped, and beaten. I didn't cry out to God at the time, or to anyone, so I was constantly running away from home. I would be picked up by the police each time, and they would take me down the station where my mom was contacted. She would pick me up from there.

In 2006, I was diagnosed with scoliosis, a spinal defect. I had to get surgery. I now have ten metal screws and two long plates supporting my spine. God still is good to me because I am still walking, running, dancing, and praising! The surgery was hard. My blood count was extremely low afterward. So I was diagnosed with anemia, a blood disorder.

Going through all this was very discouraging. At the time, I had unknowingly invited a suicidal spirit. I tried to take my life countless times because I would look back on my life and think about the amount of love this life has shown me. Clearly, the deceiving devil tried to take me out repeatedly.

God saw differently. He still somehow saw the best in me. He heard the prayers of family members and friends asking Him to keep His hands on me. I'm in thankful bliss of them to this day. My uncle introduced me to the Gospel at a young age. I was baptized at twelve years old. My spirit had accepted Jesus Christ as my Lord and Savior, but my flesh was not ready to live it at that time.

What I can say is that all that Christ has saved me from, I was able to accomplish much. In 2017, I published my first book, *Little Jesus Moment.* A Gospel book for children, kindly and softly introducing Jesus Christ to them. I appeared on multiple television shows, such as BET's *106 n Park* and *America's Got Talent.* I was able to travel across the US to perform and sing on different stages. I also made it to the Junior Olympics in track and field for the four-hundred-meter run and the four-by-four-hundred-meter relay. All before the age of thirty-one.

As I get older, I realize more and more that Jesus's blood has protected me, and I strongly believe He has more plans He wants to manifest in my favor, and that's why I'm still alive to tell my testimony. I have a six-year-old son whose wisdom and discernment are greatly monitored and supported by the Holy Spirit; it scares me sometimes. He also keeps me strong and on my toes. Knowing how cruel this world can be, I introduced Jesus Christ to my son when he was still in my belly. I will pray over him like those who prayed over me, if not more.

I will continue to give God all the glory and praise, no matter what the devil brings my way. I have all the ingredients I need to prevail! I will continue to prevail in Jesus's name. "As far as me and my house, we will serve the Lord" (Joshua 24:2).

In closing, I would like to say a prayer for the reader.

Dear Heavenly Father,

First of all, I want to give You *all* the glory and praise. It all belongs to You, Lord. You have brought us through so much, and we want to take the time to simply say, "Thank You, and we love You." Thank You for loving us, for protecting us, and for seeing the *best* in us. Thank You for sending Your only Son to die for us just so we can live again, Father God. Jesus, I would like to pray prosperity over whoever reads this book. May You provide protection, more love, clearer guidance, and understanding. I pray You shower this reader with wisdom and discernment. May You continue to shower Your precious grace and mercy on us as we also ask for You to forgive our sins and worldly desires. May You please stay near us and allow us to hear You more loudly and clearly, Lord. May we continue to put You first before every thought, every step, and every plan we come up with. May we stand together and cancel all the devil's plans and requests against us in the name of Jesus. Thank You, Lord, for what we already have. Thank You in advance for everything You have for us, for we *will* receive it in the mighty and *matchless* name of *Jesus Christ, our Lord and Savior.*

Amen.

NOTES

NOTES

NOTES

NOTES

NOTES

ABOUT THE AUTHOR

Nanette- Michelle Smith grew up in the city of Compton, California. She was baptized at the age of 12 when she gave her life over to Jesus Christ. Having a stressful time growing up in a challenging neighborhood, Nanette found it more at ease when turning her life over to Jesus Christ our Lord and Savior and she would like to share that unforgettable feeling to the world. To let the world know, no matter what situation you're in or what you've done, Jesus saves.